MEN-AT-ARMS SERIES

EDITOR: MARTIN WINDROW

The Royal Air Force
1939-45

Text by ANDREW CORMACK

Colour plates by RON VOLSTAD

OSPREY PUBLISHING LONDON

Published in 1990 by
Osprey Publishing Ltd
59 Grosvenor Street, London W1X 9DA
© Copyright 1990 Osprey Publishing Ltd

British Library Cataloguing in Publication Data
Cormack, Andrew
   The Royal Air Force, 1939–45.— (Men-at-arms: 225)
   1. Great Britain, Royal Air Force. Military
equipment, Uniforms. Military Equipment &
Uniforms history
   I. Title   II. Volstal, Ron III.   Series
358.4180941

   ISBN 0-85045-966-4

Filmset in Great Britain
Printed through Bookbuilders Ltd, Hong Kong

Acknowledgements
I would like to record my thanks to my colleagues at
the Royal Air Force Museum, Hendon and
particularly to those at the RAFM Reserve Collection
and Restoration Centre, Cardington. Assistance has
also been received from the RAF Regiment Museum,
Catterick; the Imperial War Museum; the Royal
Signals Museum; the Sikorski Institute; and the
Hawkinge Battle of Britain Museum. I am most
grateful for the help and encouragement of the
following individuals: Miss D. B. Crofts, PMRAFNS,
Messrs. J. Tomankiewicz, K. King, J. A. Chambers,
R. Dennis, Wg. Cdr. A. Barwood, P. D. Cormack and
my wife, Helen.

Artist's Note
Readers may care to note that the original paintings
from which the colour plates in this book were
prepared are available for private sale. All
reproduction copyright whatsoever is retained by the
publisher. All enquiries should be addressed to:
   Ronald B. Volstad
   P.O. Box 2730
   Canmore, Alberta,
   TOL OMO, Canada
The publishers regret that they can enter into no
correspondence upon this matter.

For a catalogue of all books published by Osprey Military
please write to:

**The Marketing Manager, Consumer Catalogue Department
Osprey Publishing Ltd, 59 Grosvenor Street, London, W1X 9DA**

Introduction

During the middle years of the Second World War the Royal Air Force constituted the only section of the British armed forces in Europe which was routinely on the offensive. Its aircraft and operations have been voluminously dealt with by historians; but its uniform and flying clothing have received only moderate attention.

This account of the 'kit' has been compiled from surviving examples in the collection of the Royal Air Force Museum, Hendon, from photographs, Air Publications—the RAF's technical manuals— and from Air Ministry Orders. The latter are a most fruitful source of information, though they are not an accurate pinpoint for the date at which any particular garment was introduced. Scrutiny of photographs of known date will often reveal clothing being worn which was not announced in AMOs until some months later. Conversely, some AMOs include indications of the supply situation and projected availability dates. It is therefore rarely possible to state exactly when particular pieces of kit were first issued.

Whereas service on the ground in Europe and the tropics definitely required different clothing, this was not necessarily the case with airborne operations. The RAF did not therefore have a set of flying clothing for home service and another for Middle or Far East use. Naturally, aircrew operating during the day at low altitude in North Africa did not need to wear as much as those flying at high altitude at night over northern Europe. Nevertheless there was a surprising commonality of flying clothing across all theatres of war and indeed across most operational rôles, although certain items were more likely to be worn by some crews than others—heated clothing, for instance, was if not the exclusive preserve of Bomber Command, at least far more common in that force than elsewhere.

During the re-armament period of the late 1930s the RAF concentrated its energies on the modernisation of its aircraft, and almost no progress was made in adapting uniform or flying clothing for active service conditions. Changes did take place in 1936, but the uniform that emerged was no more practical in operational terms than its predecessor. Apart from the introduction of the Irvin

Flying Officer Bobby Sweeney, Assistant Adjutant of 71 (Eagle) Squadron, the first RAF unit staffed by American personnel. The badge was only worn by officers and was introduced by AMOA818 of October 1940. (Courtesy Diana Barnato Walker)

Suit, which was by no means intended to become a universal flying garment, no significant modification to flying kit took place before the war began. In the light of the major changes to operational procedure necessitated by a wholesale revision of tactics, particularly in Bomber Command, this was probably a good thing; but it did mean that until such operational experience could be evaluated and the new kit designed and manufactured the aircrews were obliged to soldier on without the 'tools' to do the job. Apart from the Spitfire, the Hurricane and the Wellington the same consideration applied equally to the force's aircraft.

Part of this reluctance to change to a more practical look in uniform terms was a deep-rooted desire not to look like the Army, a tendency which manifested itself in the Air Ministry's clothing policy as frequently as the Depression years would allow. The war forced upon the Ministry the realisation that it was swimming against an irre-

The brand new Airmen's Service Dress Pattern 1936 worn by the RAF Turnhouse Detachment in the Coronation Parade 1937. Review Order with Belts, Waist, Adjustable from the 1925 Ptn. webbing equipment. (Courtesy E. Armitage, Esq.)

War Service Dress, 1944, worn by (L to R) Flt. Lt. Stainbury, DFC*, Wg. Cdr. Gibson, DFC, and Sqdn. Ldr. Villa, DFC. (RAFM PO18729)

Review Order with greatcoats, 1942. The differences between the officers' and the Airmen's coats is easily discernible. American A-16 rifles are carried and two black airmen appear half-way down the column. (Author's collection)

sistible tide, and by 1943 it had succumbed to the inevitable.

It might be said, however, that by that date the RAF had come of age and had proved that it was, if not a war-winning force in its own right, at least an indispensable element of offensive strategy. It had maintained the pressure on the Axis powers, through the flexibility of air power, during a period when the two senior services, at least in Europe, had been unable to do so. Its services to the cause and not its appearance would henceforth declare its separate, independent status.

The Commonwealth or Allied European reader of this book will look in vain through its pages for a detailed account of the uniforms of his country's participants in the air war; their flying clothing was, of course, RAF issue kit. Limitations of space have obliged the author reluctantly to include only the briefest notes on the distinctions added by some countries to basic RAF dress. A cursory and incomplete glance at the non-RAF uniforms of the Australians, South Africans and Free French, to name but a few, would serve neither the readers' purpose nor the author's but, more importantly, it would fail to give to all the countries involved that credit which their gallantry and sacrifice merits. It is hoped that this book will encourage a study of their uniforms in the near future.

Uniforms of the Royal Air Force

The last major change in the uniforms of the RAF before the outbreak of war occurred in the spring of 1936 when breeches, puttees and high collars disappeared and the service adopted the dress which it was to use until 1943.

Service Dress

The traditional blue-grey peaked cap with black mohair band bore a fabric peak for officers and a leather peak for NCOs and airmen. Officers' badges had a gilt eagle with gold embroidered crown and laurel leaves, whilst airmen had the crowned RAF monogram wreathed, all in gilding metal. Warrant officers used a gilt metal version of the officers' badge. Air Ministry Order A93/36 had introduced a Field Service cap of blue-grey (hereafter, 'BG') material on which airmen used their ordinary cap badge and officers and warrant officers carried a gilt eagle with crown above. In December 1939 the round cap was withdrawn from all non-commissioned ranks, with the exception of Police, MT Drivers and Apprentices, and throughout the war the Field Service cap reigned supreme. Berets were first introduced to the RAF Regiment in 1943, and gradually spread from trade to trade thereafter, though they were not universally adopted until after the war. Badges as for FS caps were worn on the berets.

Senior officers' SD caps from 1932 had black leather peaks with gold oak leaf embroidery: one row for group captains and two for air commodores and above. Group captains used the ordinary officers' cap badge, but air officers (i.e. ranks equivalent to Army general officers) had a gold embroidered wreath, crown and lion overlaid with a gilt eagle. A special FS cap with pale blue piped edges was introduced by AMO A142/40 and a smaller version of the Air Officers' cap badge was worn with it.

Steel helmets issued to all ranks of the RAF were ordered to be painted dark grey (AMO N1074/41).

In 1936 all non-commissioned ranks adopted a style of jacket similar to that which officers had always worn. Single breasted with four buttons and a fabric belt, it had flapped pockets in breast and skirt, and lapels. All officers' pockets had buttons, but only the breast pockets on airmen's jackets were so equipped. Trousers were worn with black footwear: boots without toecaps for airmen, and shoes with toecaps for officers. As the war progressed the issue of shoes was extended to airmen, though all ranks always maintained at least one pair of boots.

Shirts with separate collars were bright pale blue for officers and dull BG for NCOs and airmen. Ties for all ranks were black.

Officers' and warrant officers' kit was made of barathea, a soft, flat twill-like material; NCOs and airmen wore serge.

Greatcoats for all ranks were long and double breasted, the officers' version having five rows of buttons, the airmen's only four rows. In addition officers had a fabric belt and gilt buckle, three

Air and ground crews of 252 Squadron, Cyprus 1944. They wear a mixture of War Service Dress, Heavy Duty Dress, Khaki Drill and BG Service Dress. Three of the men already sport the ribbon of the Africa Star. (Courtesy A. S. Bates, Esq.)

small cuff buttons, and shoulder boards bearing rank lace. Flapped pockets cut on the slant appeared in the skirts, and there was a long rear vent. Warrant officers used the officers' pattern coat, but made of a plain cloth; officers' coats were made of fleece cloth until 1942 and melton thereafter, NCOs' and airmen's coats were serge. All ranks wore them buttoned up with the collar hooked together, or with the top buttons unfastened and the lapels turned back, according to the Orders of the Day.

Badges

Various badges appeared on this clothing; and while numerous examples are mentioned or shown in the illustrations, an exhaustive survey is not possible within the space available.

Ranks below warrant officer always wore shoulder eagles of pale blue on blue-black patches. NCOs' rank distinctions took the normal form of chevrons—three for sergeants and two for corporals—with the addition of a gilt crown above for flight sergeants. Leading aircraftmen wore a twin blade propeller badge on the upper arm. Badges indicating trades or skills were worn above rank insignia on the right sleeve only. The medical and dental trade badges were worn on the collar. Warrant officers wore the Royal Arms embroidered in pale blue on blue-black patches above the cuff. Rank and shoulder eagle badges were worn on greatcoats but not trade badges.

Officers' rank insignia appeared in the form of rings of black lace, showing a pale blue central stripe, around the cuff according to the following table. The width of the lace in inches was Broad 2 ins., Common $\frac{9}{16}$ in. and Narrow $\frac{1}{4}$ in.:

Working Blue with woollen additions courtesy of the RAF Comforts Committee have to suffice for this Whitley engine fitter, 1940. (RAFM CEB 173/24)

Squadron leaders wore their narrow lace between the two common ones. Rank insignia was worn on both sleeves of the Service Dress. Trade badges were not worn by officers and WOs with the exception of those designating branches, viz. medical, dental, education and chaplains. The uniform of the latter was Service Dress but worn with a black cassock-waistcoat and white clerical collar. Their cap badge was a cross pattée crowned with the RAF monogram in the centre.

Aircrews were distinguished by brevets or half-wings. The pilots' and observers' badges had been in use since 1918, but the burgeoning of aircrews and their skills gave rise to new brevets as follows:

	B	C	N
Marshal of the RAF	1	4	
Air Chief Marshal	1	3	
Air Marshal	1	2	
Air Vice-Marshal	1	1	
Air Commodore	1		
Group Captain		4	
Wing Commander		3	
Squadron Leader		2	1
Flight Lieutenant		2	
Flying Officer		1	
Pilot Officer			1

Trade	Symbol	Introduced
Air Gunner	AG	21.12.39
Observer Radio	RO	29.5.41
Air Bomber	B	17.9.42
Navigator	N	17.9.42
Flight Engineer	E	17.9.42
Wireless Operator	S	2.12.43
Meteorological Observer	M	26.4.45

Two rare photographs of colonial shoulder titles in use. A number of unofficial examples are known from contemporary pictures, this West Indies title among them. (Courtesy M. Philpotts)

Japanese weaponry is collected up under the supervision of FO Gogarthy, RAF Regiment. Jungle Green combat kit is worn without Regiment badges. Note the sandals of the man second from left. (RAFM/RAF Regt.)

Up to December 1939 Air Gunners had worn the brass winged bullet arm badge granted them in 1923. The rather odd title 'Observer Radio', which confusingly appeared as Radio Operator in AMO A402/41, was the Air Ministry's disguise for the new secret trade of Radar Operator. The RO brevet was quickly replaced by the Navigator badge and the trade was redesignated Navigator (Radio) by AMO A1019/42. Wireless Operators were always trained as Air Gunners and wore that brevet until the Signaller brevet was introduced.

A further badge which was awarded only to aircrews of 8 Group, Pathfinder Force was introduced in November 1942. It consisted of a small gilt eagle worn on the flap of the left breast pocket.

Those men who had joined the Auxiliary Air Force or the RAF Volunteer Reserve before the war were distinguished by 'A' and 'VR' badges; officers wore them in gilt metal on the collars of their jackets and the shoulder boards of their greatcoats, while airmen's badges appeared in embroidered form below their shoulder eagles. 'VR' badges were abolished in mid-1943.

By October of that year it had become evident that a fundamental change in kit was required, and War Service Dress was introduced (AMO A1062). The garments had in fact been in use since 1940 under the designation Suits, Aircrew and they are described in the Flying Clothing section. There was no difference in quality or cut between officers' or airmen's garments, and the jacket was usually worn with collar and tie, the top two buttons being left undone to form a lapel. Rank, shoulder eagles, trade and flying badges were worn by other ranks in exactly the same way as on Service Dress. Officers wore rank lace on their shoulder straps. It was specifically stated that WSD was a working dress and was not to be worn for parades or when off station.

The expansion of the RAF into fields which had never before been its concern, particularly airfield defence, prompted the advent of Heavy Duty Dress which came to be used not only by the RAF Regiment but by personnel serving in Iceland, forward areas in the Middle East, the Airfield Construction Service, Embarkation Units, Combined Operations personnel and the aircrews of Second Tactical Air Force amongst others. Heavy Duty Dress was the RAF's title for Army khaki

A fine study of a Polish group captain wearing RAF cuff and PAF collar rank insignia, the distinctive Observer 1st Class flying badge, and the PAF Staff College badge, 1946. (Courtesy Gp. Capt. Gogolinski-Elan)

Battledress, and was worn with ordinary BG rank, trade and shoulder badges by NCOs and airmen and with shoulder strap rank lace by officers. Air Ministry Order A251/42 stipulated that NCOs and airmen should wear the jacket fastened to the neck, but officers and warrant officers wore theirs open with blue collars and black ties. In January 1944 khaki shirts were permitted for the Regiment only.

In bad weather BG greatcoats were worn with this khaki kit in the UK, but for service overseas khaki greatcoats were issued, though worn with RAF badges and buttons (AMO N69/44). On the introduction of HDD to the Regiment BG webbing was withdrawn and replaced with drab 1937 Pattern which must have been worn even when parading in BG Service Dress. On exercises and active service the Regiment and RAF glider pilots used denims to save wear on their HDD. On this

Crews of No. 3 Armoured Car Company pose in comic mode during a brew-up, 1939. Dark blue overalls over SD with sweaters are worn along with mixed webbing Ptns. 1908 and 1925 and Goggles, Motor Transport. (Author's collection)

Struggling to mount the defensive armament of a Whitley Mk I, this Polish armourer wears the old high collar 1919 Pattern jacket. The flight sergeant has been issued with an SD cap due to clothing shortages, this item having been withdrawn from the RAF. The British warrant officer keeps a beady eye on his foreign trainee. (RAFM CEB 174/14)

clothing officers' rank lace appeared on both shoulders, but NCOs and LACs wore their rank badges on the right sleeve only (AMO N72/42).

Middle East and Far East

Since its inception the RAF had served in the Middle East and India and had developed its own khaki drill clothing which had been modernised in 1936 along the lines of Home Service wear. All jackets were therefore of the lapelled type, and were worn with khaki rank badges (by NCOs) and red shoulder eagles. Trade and leading aircraftmen badges were also red. Warrant officers wore the officers' style jacket with pointed cuffs, but without shoulder straps, and used a gilding metal Royal Arms badge instead of an embroidered one. The officers' jacket had shoulder boards which bore rank lace.

All ranks wore trousers or shorts as occasion

RAF Regiment personnel being inspected outside Jerusalem, 1945. Note the pistol lanyards looped up to the rear of the waist belts to make them less easy to steal. Short puttees are worn; and there is no sign of any shoulder titles. (RAFM/RAF Regt.)

demanded, and in addition to the Home Service headgear Wolseley helmets and/or pith hats were available; airmen were not issued with the former in India. Both helmets were fitted with puggarees bearing the RAF flash on the left. Khaki shirts were of the short-sleeved, collar-attached bush type, and when worn without the jacket, officers' rank lace appeared on the shoulder straps. On NCOs' and airmen's bush shirts white tape chevrons were used, though the LACs retained their red propeller. Flight sergeants' crowns were represented by a white square. No shoulder eagles were worn. WOs wore their badge on a brown leather strap on the right wrist only. Bush shirts developed into jackets during the war, acquiring pockets in the skirts, a belt and, usually, large black plastic buttons. Ties and footwear were black as for Home Service, though brown leather or suede shoes were permitted to officers in 1944 (AMO A898). Long khaki stockings were worn with shorts.

In 1925 the RAF had introduced its own unique pattern of BG webbing equipment for UK service whilst retaining drab 1908 Pattern for overseas use. After September 1939 the '25 Pattern set was used in France and the tropics, but it was abandoned in 1941 when a BG version of the 1937 Pattern set was introduced. As it was possible to mix and match elements of the two sets, particularly the pistol equipment, the two patterns ran in tandem throughout the war.

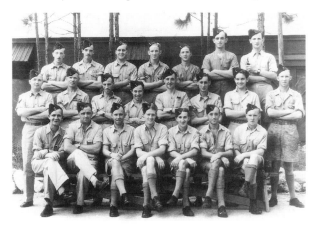

Ground crews at Windsor Field, Nassau, Bahamas, 1944. Most wear shirts and shorts but some sport the collarless, short leg/sleeve tropical combination overall. (RAFM DB 39)

The Women's Auxiliary Air Force

The WAAF was formed on 28 June 1939 from the Royal Air Force Companies of the Auxiliary Territorial Service. Air Ministry Order A578 of August 1940 declared its purpose to be 'the substitution of women for RAF personnel in certain appointments and trades throughout the RAF'. Initially these trades were selected from the administrative, clerical and domestic side of the RAF's organisation, but gradually more operational rôles were filled, and by the end of the war the WAAF participated in 89 trades.

Although uniform had been approved by September 1939 its issue was intermittent until the spring of 1940. Officers' and airwomen's caps differed considerably in shape, the former being more oval and made up of three sections in the crown, the latter rather like a mob cap gathered into a band all of one piece. Both featured a false rear peak of BG fabric, but otherwise bore the same distinctions—band, peak and badge—as their RAF equivalents. Late in 1941 the special oak leaf peak lace and the air officers' cap badge was conceded to Group and Air officers, and black patent leather peaks therefore appeared on their caps.

Account being taken of the female figure, WAAF jackets were nevertheless basically the same as those of their male colleagues, though airwomen wore a soft, barathea-like fabric, not serge. On the 1940 Pattern jacket all pockets bore buttons, but after October 1943 those on the lower pockets were dispensed with (AMO N1108). Officers carried cuff rank lace in the same manner as the RAF, but they were known by different titles (RAF equivalents in brackets): Commandant in Chief (AM or above), Air Chief Commandant (AVM), Air Commandant (A.Cdre), Group, Wing, Squadron, Flight and Section Officers (Gp.Capt. to FO), Assistant Section Officer (PO).

All WAAF officers bore gilt metal 'A's on their lapels in recognition of their auxiliary status. Non-

Flying Officer Gulliver in bush jacket and shorts, India, 1945. The buttons are probably of the segmented leather sports jacket type while the buckle is gilt metal. (Courtesy H. Gulliver, Esq.)

Ground crews of 605 Squadron, Palembang, 1942. Uniformity has been sacrificed to comfort and protection during the retreat from Singapore. (RAFM DB 435)

commissioned officers and airwomen wore embroidered 'A's below their shoulder eagles, though these badges seem to have become rarer as the war progressed, probably as a result of the change from volunteer to conscripted membership after the National Service Act No. 2 of December 1941. The rank insignia of WAAF NCOs was described in AMO A212/40: senior sergeants, sergeants and corporals wore the same badges as their RAF counterparts; under officers wore pale blue embroidered crowns with red cushions within an open laurel wreath, also pale blue, on both cuffs. AMO A578/40 noted that no under officers had been appointed up to August that year, and that there was no WAAF equivalent of leading aircraftman, and therefore no propeller badge.

These badges and titles underwent a drastic change in January 1942 when AMO A104 announced that both would henceforth fall into line with RAF practice, and that the WAAF would include leading aircraftwomen with the appropriate propeller badge. Furthermore, under officers were abolished and WAAF warrant officers were to wear the same cap and rank badges as their RAF equivalents and could substitute brown leather gloves for BG knitted ones. These changes,

Greatcoat Order for Dame Mary Welch and a party of WAAFs, 1944. Note the differences in shape between the officer's and the airwomen's caps and coats. (RAFM DB 179)

Pilots of 605 Squadron, Palembang, January 1942. Any semblance of regular flying kit has almost disappeared from this group. The figure at far right appears to be wearing a thin leather jacket with cuffs; his colleague probably wears a black cotton flying overall. (RAFM DB 435)

again the result of the National Service Act No. 2, brought the WAAF within the framework of RAF law as regards discipline and liabilities.

The skirts worn by all ranks were plain, straight, without pleats, and to a regulation length of between 14 and 16 inches from the ground. Grey Lisle stockings were worn with flat, black lace-up shoes. Ties were black and shirts pale blue for officers and BG for airwomen, although it appears to have been quite common for officers' style shirts to have been worn by NCOs.

After the ill-clad winter of 1939 officers and airwomen wore double breasted BG greatcoats with five buttons in each row, the officers' version being identical to that of RAF officers but with soft, sewn-in shoulder straps rather than detachable boards. Rank insignia was worn as in the RAF, along with shoulder eagles for airwomen, though while officers continued to wear gilt 'A's on their shoulder straps, embroidered 'A's were not supplied with airwomen's greatcoats. Before December 1940 WAAFs had been issued with a BG double breasted raincoat on which rank appeared but not eagles, but this garment was withdrawn when greatcoats were issued. Some WAAFs seem to have retained raincoats well into the war, and they were also issued to WAAF Police instead of oilskins (A587/44).

It seems to have been realised quicker in the

WAAF than in the RAF that protective clothing was required for everyday work, and early kit scales included white and blue overall coats, blue combination suits and separate dark blue cotton jackets and trousers for certain trades. By late 1941 outdoor and dirty trades were issued with 'Suits, Working, Serge', which was BG Battledress by another name. Rank badges were worn on these suits but not often does one see eagles. Shirts and ties could be replaced or covered by BG sweaters, and this dress was often seen with gloves or gauntlets and ankle or wellington boots with white socks.

Slacks of dark blue material, not BG, had been an issue item during the period of *ad hoc* kitting in the early days, but when proper uniform became available they were withdrawn. Obviously this deprived some girls who were not entitled by their

Airwomen Fowler and Camphill, Gloucester, 1942. Airwomen's caps tended to be a law unto the wearer! (Courtesy Mrs A. J. Hamilton née Camphill)

trade to Suits, Working, Serge of a very useful garment, and AMO N1365 of November '41 reintroduced them 'as a protection against damp and cold only when taking shelter from air raids'. It is certain that they were more widely used and were worn not only in conjunction with overalls, but with the Service Dress jacket. AMO A417/42 permitted officers to purchase slacks for air raid shelter wear only.

As the war progressed the wearing of trousers by WAAFs of all trades increased though they were always regarded as on-station working clothing. By 1945 it was also authorised for girls to wear the short jacket of the SWS with their working skirt, thereby mixing Service and Working Dress.

WAAF officers were not included in the regulations governing the issue of Suits, Working, Serge and they were not officially permitted to wear them until December 1942 (AMO A1331), when their use was sanctioned for Balloon Site Supervisors and Equipment Officers. An extension to all officers was made in March 1944. Rank lace appeared on shoulder straps which had to be specially added to officers' jackets.

It took the Air Ministry a long time to concede that all WAAFs required something in which to carry everyday necessities apart from their gas mask haversacks, which were regularly packed with items having little to do with chemical warfare. In March 1944 (AMO A289) a zipped shoulder bag of BG barathea was introduced for officers, but airwomen did not receive the same concession until June 1945 (AMO N647) when their bag was produced in black serge.

Overseas dress

The WAAF Regulations outlined in AMO A578/40 declared that the force was to be available for service overseas. During 1940 small numbers of officers served in staff appointments in the USA, and from 1941 larger numbers were posted to the Middle East. Airwomen did not go abroad *en masse* until 1944, but a substantial contingent was recruited locally in Kenya and Palestine from 1943 onwards; NCOs were posted to this force from the UK. In 1944 airwomen were sent not only to the Middle East but to India as well, and followed the invasion forces to France very shortly after D-Day.

Air Ministry Order A808 of October 1941

introduced tropical clothing for officers which followed closely the style of garments worn by their male colleagues; jackets had pointed cuffs and detachable, rank-bearing shoulder boards. Skirts had a double box pleat front and rear and fell to within 15½ inches of the ground. Short-sleeved, collar-attached bush shirts were worn with rank displayed on the shoulder straps. Ties and shoes were as for Home Service, but stockings were khaki Lisle.

The headgear to be worn with this suit was the pith hat with a three-fold puggaree bearing the RAF flash on the left. In addition, because the officers were on active service, often in rear operational areas rather than offices, they were required to provide themselves with a BG haversack and waterbottle carrier with the appropriate braces. Whilst the pith hat was considered the official hot weather headgear it is certain that Service Dress caps were commonly worn in preference.

Airwomen's KD clothing may have been functional, but it was the least elegant of their uniforms. Unlike their officers the other ranks were provided with a bush jacket—a rather shapeless, open-neck, long-sleeved tunic with belt and four pockets— which was ordered to be worn as a loose fitting garment. The sleeves bore red eagles and khaki rank badges as appropriate, along with metal buckle and plastic buttons both of which were black. Plain khaki skirts, long-sleeved shirts, socks and/or Lisle stockings finished off the outfit, in conjunction with black ties and Home Service pattern shoes. In working dress the jacket was often dispensed with, and the shirt, worn open at the neck and with rolled sleeves, used in its place. KD slacks were also provided.

No special tropical headwear was issued, though Wolseley helmets were available on loan for the outward journey, and the SD cap had to suffice until May 1944 when Field Service caps were introduced with black plastic buttons and badges. FS caps had been used unofficially in the UK before this date, but AMO N429/44 specified that they were only for wear with tropical clothing. It seems that officers were not permitted to use them. Locally made sandals were allowed in place of black shoes in working dress. Airwomen were also expected to carry haversacks and waterbottles.

Overalls, Combination, Blue worn by the personnel of a barrage balloon crew taking a moment's break to listen to a Negro Spiritual. (RAFM DB 189)

Aircraftwoman 1st Class Alice Gross, Egypt, 1943. Note the ample cut and the buttoning style of the KD slacks. (Courtesy Alice Gross)

Princess Mary's Royal Air Force Nursing Service

The Royal Air Force possessed its own nursing service from its earliest days; in 1923 it gained its Royal patron, and the members became familiarly known as 'PM's. Initially members held 'appointments' and were controlled on behalf of the RAF by their own Medical Board, the advice of which the Air Ministry always accepted. The hierarchical structure was therefore solely medical and in 1939 was composed of a matron-in-chief, matrons, senior sisters, sisters and staff nurses.

These appointments were indicated on uniform by single bands of cuff lace; maroon for matrons and senior sisters, dark blue for sisters and staff nurses. The lace of the three senior appointments bore a pale blue centre stripe, whilst that of staff nurses was plain. Matrons' lace was $1\frac{1}{2}$ ins. wide with a $\frac{1}{2}$ in. inset, and senior sisters' and sisters' lace was $1\frac{1}{4}$ ins. with a $\frac{1}{4}$ in. inset. Garments on which lace could not be worn were fitted with shoulder boards of the appropriate colour with pale blue lace of $\frac{1}{2}$ or $\frac{1}{4}$ in. width. Staff nurses' boards were plain dark blue; the matron-in-chief wore a senior sister's lace above a matron's lace.

As a consequence of the Defence (Women's Forces) Regulations 1941 the PMs' legal status changed and they became members of the Armed Forces. With effect from 1 April 1941 staff nurses were abolished and the lowest rank was henceforth sister (A506/41). In March 1943 by AMO A196 it was announced that the PMRAFNS would wear RAF rank insignia whilst retaining their nursing titles. The following table gives the equivalent RAF ranks:

Matron-in-Chief	Air Commodore
Principal Matron	Wing Commander
Matron	Squadron Leader
Senior Sister	Flight Lieutenant
Sister	Flying Officer

These ranks were indicated in ordinary black and blue lace in exactly the same manner as in the RAF and WAAF; the colourful appointment lace and shoulder boards were discontinued.

Sisters and a matron (second from left) of Princess Mary's RAF Nursing Service: Summer Service Dress, Halton, 1930s. (RAFM/PMRAFNS Archive)

The necessity to have both a uniform and working clothing and the fact that the Service operated in hospitals and in the field, at home and abroad, gave rise to a bewildering variety of Orders of Dress.

Service Dress—Summer (May–September)

There were two variants of headgear: the black felt four-cornered hat or the BG double-peaked 'storm cap', both worn with black mohair band and officers' embroidered badge. The jacket was of Norfolk cut with buttoned belt and skirt pockets. Its most distinctive feature was a pair of broad pleats down front and back extending from hem to hem. A long plain skirt was worn to within 10 ins. of the ground and the outfit was finished with black tie, shoes and stockings and white gloves and shirt, the latter with rounded collar points.

Service Dress—Winter (October–April)

Winter clothing consisted of a coat-frock in BG barathea. This was a long-sleeved, straight dress with $1\frac{1}{2}$ in. stand collar and a false front closure of 12 small RAF half-ball buttons which concealed a press-stud opening. Narrow white lawn collar and cuffs were worn. This dress was invariably accompanied by a shoulder cape with a shallow stand collar and a large rosette at the centre rear. Headwear, even outside, was a white veil of traditional shape bearing a pale blue crowned wings badge on its centre rear corner. In bad weather it is likely that the storm cap was worn.

Appointment and later rank lace appeared on the cuffs of both jacket and dress. Jacket collars and the corners of the cape were decorated with the crowned, winged caduceus of Mercury in gilt. When worn with the dress no shoulder boards appeared on the cape.

Double breasted greatcoats of officers' pattern were included in kit scales in the late 1930s; they were worn with coloured shoulder boards or, after 1943, BG boards with rank lace.

Air Ministry Order A137/36 had introduced an optional three-buttoned cloak of arm's length which had a stand and fall collar 2 ins. deep which bore appointment colours—all maroon for matrons, edged with ¾ in. maroon or dark blue binding for senior sisters and sisters, and with plain BG collars for staff nurses. The two senior appointments had maroon silk linings to the cloak and the two juniors had powder blue linings. The medical badge appeared in the points of the collar.

As a concession to Field Service the PMs were permitted to wear the jacket of the WAAF Suit, Working, Serge with their skirts, and the storm cap was abolished, to be replaced with a BG beret with officers' cap badge.

Senior Sisters Thomas, Wilson and Keyse and Matron Hards (L. to R.) at a Buckingham Palace investiture, April 1943. Winter Service Dress with shoulder capes, head veils, white gloves, and the new rank lace. (RAFM/PMRAFNS Archive)

Ward Dress—Home and Overseas Service

Daily nursing duties were performed in a white cotton drill dress of medium weight fastening at the front with 14 small domed mother-of-pearl buttons. It had a turn-over collar with round corners, a three-button belt, two skirt pockets and elbow length sleeves. Detachable lower sleeves were provided, as were loops on the shoulders to carry boards. It was worn with white veil, opaque stockings and laced buckskin or canvas shoes. In Europe, except when actually treating patients, the BG shoulder cape was worn adorned with appointment or rank boards; the white dress collar was turned over the cape collar. Matrons always wore the coat-frock as their indoor working dress for Home Service.

Tropical Uniform Dress

In hot countries matrons wore a long white coat-frock of Tricoline with long sleeves, side belts, a front opening of 12 pearl buttons and a roll step collar. The collar and cuffs were trimmed with plain white silk braid.

Senior sisters and lower ranks wore white cotton dresses with long sleeves, 14-button front openings and a false modelled-in belt. A 3 in. collar was worn open with a slight turnback lapel. There were no visible pockets and, it seems, no provision for status or rank insignia.

All ranks had the alternative of a white solar helmet with the underside of the brim coloured blue, or an elegant white felt Panama type hat, both of which were embellished with RAF flashes on the left side of the puggaree or band. Stockings and shoes were white, the latter of suede.

Unlike the WAAF the PMs had always had a Mess Dress, which followed closely the lines of the Tropical Uniform Dresses but was made in BG or white silk for winter or summer respectively. As Mess Dress had been suspended for the RAF in 1939 it is presumed that its use was also discontinued by the PMs for the duration of the war.

Sir Archibald Sinclair, the Air Minister (left), with a matron and medical officer at an RAF hospital in Cairo, 1942. Compare the matron's dress with those of the sisters in the next photograph. (RAFM/PMRAFNS Archive)

The Allies

By 1940 Great Britain stood alone against the Third Reich, but within her shores she had acquired large reserves of foreign manpower eager to take up the struggle to reclaim their lost homelands. She was also fortunate in the generous response of her Empire in the mother country's hour of need. Canada, Australia, New Zealand and South Africa had small air forces of their own before the war, and although the Canadian and New Zealand uniforms were similar to those of the RAF there were sufficient differences to warrant their being treated separately elsewhere. The uniforms of Australia and South Africa were completely different. The Dominions also tended to supply whole units for service alongside the RAF, though naturally there were substantial numbers of individuals serving permanently or temporarily with British squadrons.

The colonies which had no air forces of their own supplied valuable contributions of manpower to the RAF, and their personnel were always distinguished by shoulder titles, these usually being rectangular black for NCOs and airmen and

Two patterns of nursing dresses, one with open neck and medical collar badges, the other with buttons up to the neck and no badges. Both have the three-button belt. (RAFM/PMRAFNS Archive)

Country	Date	AMO
Rhodesia	10.40	A760
Canada	3.41	A219
Australia	,,	,,
New Zealand	,,	,,
South Africa	,,	,,
Newfoundland	7.41	A563
Aden	12.42	A1303
Bahamas	,,	,,
Barbados	,,	,,
Basutoland	,,	,,
Bechuanaland	,,	,,
Bermuda	,,	,,
British Guiana	,,	,,
British Honduras	,,	,,
Ceylon	,,	,,
Cyprus	,,	,,
Falkland Islands	,,	,,
Fiji	,,	,,
Gambia	,,	,,
Gibraltar	,,	,,
Gold Coast	,,	,,
Hong Kong	,,	,,
Jamaica	,,	,,
Kenya	,,	,,
Leeward Islands	,,	,,
Malaya	,,	,,
Malta	,,	,,
Mauritius	,,	,,
Nigeria	,,	,,
Nyasaland	,,	,,
Palestine	,,	,,
Seychelles	,,	,,
Sierra Leone	,,	,,
Somaliland Protectorate	,,	,,
Swaziland	,,	,,
Tanganyika	,,	,,
Trinidad	,,	,,
Uganda	,,	,,
Windward Islands	,,	,,
Zanzibar	,,	,,
India	2.45	A163
Burma	,,	,,

curved BG for officers, bearing the name of the country of origin in pale blue embroidery. For tropical kit the titles appeared in red on KD. Whilst the official list of such titles is long a number of unofficial additions are known.

The same procedure was adopted by many of the Allied European nations, though the Free French Air Force wore completely different uniforms, and the Poles made greater additions to their RAF kit than did most others.

The following is a list of the Empire titles with their dates of introduction and authorising order:

In the immediate post-fall of France period the Allies were equipped as well as British clothing stocks would allow, but some continued to use their old national uniforms and others received pre-1936 RAF kit which was still available in small quantities. The Czechs, Belgians, Poles, Norwegians, Danes and Dutch all adopted RAF clothing and a brief résumé of the early distinctions worn on it is contained in AMO A95/41. Eventually most of the governments in exile adapted it so as to resemble their pre-war clothing.

The Czechs and Belgians simply added shoulder titles, which were announced in AMO A555/40. They also wore their own flying badges, on the right breast pocket for the Czechs and above the left breast pocket for the Belgians. The few Danish Army Air Service officers who reached England served in either RAF or Norwegian Air Force units, but were only granted a shoulder title by AMO A744 of August 1944, perhaps as a result of being stung into action by the Luxembourg authorities, who had claimed similar distinctions for their three serving airmen in March (AMO N292).

Poland

Initially the Poles, who provided the largest Allied contingent (17,000 personnel in 14 squadrons), contented themselves with shoulder titles and a new cap badge—the Polish eagle on an Amazonian shield—in silver metal for NCOs and airmen and, with added Hussar wings, in gold and silver embroidery for officers, who also wore a similar badge on their left breast pockets. On FS caps officers wore the ordinary RAF officers' badge, though later they acquired a silver Polish style one like the airmen. RAF flying badges were used.

During the winter of 1940/41 the status of Polish forces in the UK was put on to a more independent footing, and the resultant uniform changes were announced in AMO A413 of 5 June 1941, having come into operation from 1 March. Shoulder eagles were removed from airmen's jackets and greatcoats; flight sergeants replaced their crowns with small buttons; and warrant officers acquired a new cuff badge consisting of a black, circular cushion 2 ins. in diameter, trimmed with pale blue russia braid and bearing centrally a small uniform button. All buttons henceforth bore the Polish eagle. Shoulder titles became BG and of curved design for all ranks.

While RAF rank badges continued to be worn on the sleeves, PAF collar rank badges also appeared on clothing. These were small, rectangular patches of BG cloth with pointed upper ends. The senior officers' versions bore single gold bars of zig-zag generals' embroidery with three, two or one stars for generals (ACM), generals of division (AM) or generals of brigade (AVM). There was no Polish equivalent of air commodore, though Poles were appointed as RAF air commodores. Colonels, lieutenant-colonels and majors each had two plain bars and three, two and one stars respectively. Captains, lieutenants and second lieutenants had three, two and one gold stars only. It was almost always the case that the PAF insignia did not show the exact RAF equivalent which appeared on the cuff because the RAF had not accepted officers on the basis of their PAF rank, but had down-graded them by one or two positions.

In March 1944 a slight modification was made to the senior officers' insignia in that brigadiers' patches were bestowed on air commodores and divisional and full generals' patches were allotted to AVMs and AMs. This reflected the fact that no Polish officer had attained the rank of general/ACM.

NCOs' and airmen's patches followed a similar system, those for warrant officers and flight sergeants being traced on the sides and point with narrow gold lace and bearing a gold star and two chevrons respectively. Sergeants had one chevron without tracing; corporals, LACs and ACs 1st Class had three, two and one lateral bars in gold; AC 2s had no patches. NCOs or airmen undergoing officer training had their patches edged in red and white silk cord and, on completion of their courses, this was replaced with silver tracing during the probationary period before commissioning. Those who had either completed their training in France or had started it there during the winter of 1939–40 held the anomalous rank of 'aspirant' until commissioned, which was designated by a silver traced patch with a longitudinal gold stripe. In 1943 for reasons of economy the badges were produced for other ranks in yellow and white machine embroidery instead of gold and silver lace.

The year 1941 also saw the introduction of flying badges of traditional Polish design featuring a swooping eagle holding in its beak a laurel wreath and in its claws one or more lightning bolts. The following table indicates the variations according to aircrew function:

Trade	Colour Gold or Silver	Thunderbolts	Notes
Pilot	S	None	
Observer	G	3	
Air Gunner	G	None	Pre '42
Wireless Operator/Air Gunner	G	I	'42–'44
Flight Engineer	S	None	silver cog in right claw
Radar Operator	G	2	'42–'44

Bomb Aimers used either the observers' or air gunners' badges; navigators used the observers badge.

In 1944 modifications were made to these badges to make the functions they represented more obvious by means of letters superimposed on the wreath:

Trade	Colour	Thunderbolts	Letter	Colour
Wop/AG	G	3	R	S
AG/Signaller	G	3	S	S
Meteorological Observer	G	3	M	S
Bomb Aimer	S	None	B	G
Flight Engineer	S	None	M	G

These badges were worn high up on the left shoulder secured by a safety chain fastened under the jacket lapel.

Norway

Norwegian personnel ultimately manned five Fighter and Coastal Command squadrons. In July 1942 AMO A667 stipulated that collar rank insignia was to be worn consisting of silver stars— three for colonels and captains, two for lieutenant-colonels and lieutenants, and one for majors and second lieutenants; field officers also had the angle of the collar edged in silver lace. Major-Generals had a broad gold lace with a silver star super-imposed. NCOs and airmen wore RAF rank stripes in silver braid on BG patches on the upper arms; flight sergeants had their crowns replaced with a silver crowned shield bearing the Nor-wegian lion. LACs wore the RAF badge.

On their SD caps officers wore a badge com-posed of a cockade of white, blue, white, red (outer

Study of a Stirling bomb aimer showing the C Type helmet with G oxygen mask. Note the face sealing wire over the nose; and the quick release snap hooks on the parachute harness. (RAFM/Mildenhall Albums)

Pilot and navigator training in an Airspeed Oxford, 1940. The former wears the 1930 Pattern helmet with Mk III goggles, the latter a Type B helmet and 1930 Pattern flying suit. (RAFM CEB 172/5A)

to centre) within an open oak wreath below a winged national shield, the wreath and wings being silver wire. Generals wore gold cord chin straps, senior officers silver cord and junior officers black leather. The winged national shield appeared also on the side of the FS cap, the buttons of which were replaced by the national cockade, upper, and a gold lion on a red ground, lower. These cockades were joined by gold lace for generals and silver for officers. NCOs and airmen wore the same side badge and top cockade with a silver button below, but no linking braid.

Nationality titles within an embroidered surround were worn on the left shoulder in silver on BG for officers and white on black for other ranks. A small Norwegian flag appeared on the right shoulder.

Officers seem to have worn bronze buttons, and false pointed cuffs indicated by blue cord piping. No RAF cuff rank lace was worn. Flying badges in silver embroidery were positioned over the right breast pocket.

Holland

A small number of Dutch aviators, most of them originating from the Naval Air Service, escaped to England and served alongside the RAF. Those who did not retain their naval uniform, or who had come from the Army Air Service, wore RAF uniform with shoulder titles in the usual manner. The Army Air Service personnel continued to use their flying badges; pilots wore a gold eagle in embroidery or metal on an orange disc edged in gold; observers had a gold-winged, blue disc bearing 'W' and an edging of gold. Pilot-observers wore the pilots' badge above the observers' disc without wings. These badges appeared above the left breast pocket. It would seem that on returning to the Continent bright blue collar patches bearing stars indicating rank were introduced, but photographs as late as December 1944 do not show them and no AMO has been found announcing them.

Flying Clothing

At first sight the wide range of kit which was produced in the six years of war would seem to suggest that aircrews by 1945 could be wearing a whole jumble of equipment of various dates. In fact this did not happen, due to a number of factors. Firstly, the variety of equipment was a consequence of the search for comfort and efficiency as manifested by the performance of the kit in operational conditions. Whereas before the war there was little money for research and development, and equipment remained in service for a long time, after 1939 there was little reluctance to discard apparatus which did not perform satisfactorily.

Secondly, most of the headgear was interdependent, in that fitments of helmets to oxygen masks were specific to particular equipments, and it was almost impossible to wear, for instance, a B Type helmet with a Type G oxygen mask. Certain modifications allowed mismatched kit to be mated together, but by and large it was easier and more efficient to issue improved kit as a package rather than to adapt old to accommodate new.

Thirdly, it must be faced that the casualty rate was so high, at least in Bomber Command, that it was a lucky crewman who survived repeated periods of operations long enough to reap the benefits of the development process. New kit was therefore issued to new airmen, the old hands being no longer on the scene to enjoy the increased comfort it bestowed.

Finally, the realisation that cold was the greatest enemy led to the provision of cockpit heating so that by 1944, despite the differences in length of flights, altitudes and the times of operation—day or night—there was almost no difference in kit between a Typhoon pilot and a Lancaster navigator.

In the following description the equipment and clothing has been divided into generic types.

This Middle East Hurricane pilot clearly shows that there was no sealing capability on the Type D oxygen mask. This is the Variant 3 with the Type 21 Electro-Magnetic microphone. (Courtesy A. S. Bates, Esq.)

Wherever possible dates of service have been given, so that it is feasible to work out the ensemble that an airman could wear at any particular period. Reference should also be made to the illustrations which show 'typical' combinations of clothing for each period of the war.

Helmets

The RAF used four variants of flying helmet during the war, of which the first was the **Type B**. It was made of brown chrome leather and accommodated its telephone earpieces (10A/8543) in zipped, padded oval housings. It had a chamois leather lining, no integral wiring, a leather chin strap, and a slit back with adjustment strap, which also acted as a quick release to pull the helmet and attached oxygen mask off the head in the event of a bale-out. Press-studs for positioning the Type D oxygen mask appeared in pairs on the inside edges of the face aperture. Certain modifications to the helmet were necessary when it was used in conjunction with the Mk IV series goggles (see below).

The **Type C** helmet introduced in mid-1941 was made of the same leather, but was constructed in bands running from front to rear of the head, a cut which made it more comfortable than the 'quartered' style of its predecessor. It housed its earpieces in squat rubber cylindrical housings, and featured external press-studs on the left side, and either press-studs or a flat hook on the right, for the attachment of the oxygen mask. Goggles were retained by pairs of straps positioned above and on either side of the telephone holders with a fifth in the centre rear. The Type C was originally issued without wiring and with a leather chin strap, but by 1944 it had acquired integral wiring, elastic chin straps and re-arranged goggle retaining tabs.

The **Type D** and **Type E** helmets were announced in March 1942 and December 1944 respectively, and were essentially the same as the Type C, but made of sand-coloured cotton twill (D) or Aertex material (E). They were intended for Middle and Far East wear, but were lightweight and comfortable and therefore found greater currency in other parts of the world as well. The D featured a semi-circular neck flap as a protection against sunburn. Like the C they were initially issued unwired, but by late 1944 wired versions had appeared.

Helmets Types C, D and E were normally fitted with telephones Type 16 (10A/12401) or Type 32 (10A/13466).

Goggles

Despite the introduction of full canopies for aircraft cockpits and glazed turrets for gunners goggles still formed a vital part of aircrew equipment. Not only did they permit the wearing of tinted 'windows' (as eyepieces were called) in an effort to overcome the glare of summer or above-cloud flying, but they provided protection in case of damage to the windscreen or leakage of pressurised fluids inside the cockpit. The large size of early war examples also made them effective masks against fire. In addition, when it became quite common practice for tail gunners to remove sections of the perspex from their turrets in an attempt to improve night vision, goggles again became indispensable.

The design of goggles in the inter-war period underwent very little change, and the Mk II set, of essentially First World War origin, lasted until 1933 when the Mk III series was introduced. The **Mk III** was a simple plain window mask with padded leather surround and elasticated adjustable head strap. It was lightweight, the windows were celluloid not plexiglass, and it was easy to wear. However, the Air Ministry must have considered them unsatisfactory for in mid-1940 it announced the introduction of the **Mk IV** series, in three variants according to manufacturer.

The new pattern was a large, split-window mask made of brass in the IV and IVB variants and Bakelite in the IVA. Padding was provided by detachable, clip-on rubber pads supplied in three sizes to suit the wearer, whose face size and shape could be further accommodated by adjustment of the nose bridge. The adjustment screw also acted as the attachment point for a tinted anti-glare panel which could be raised or lowered as desired.

The designers had obviously had some difficulty in fitting the mask to the B Type helmet with its bulky earphone housings, and their solution was to provide the spring-loaded headband with large, cotton-covered loops which encircled the telephone holders. It would seem that most wearers were content to sling the goggles in place relying upon tension in the headband to keep them stable. However, so large and heavy were they that the designers provided metal plates bearing the male halves of three press-studs which could be riveted or sewn to the helmet above the earphones, and smaller plates with one stud to be mounted below the housings. These studs engaged with female press-studs attached to clips threaded onto the wire loops, thereby locking the goggles firmly on the wearer's head.

This contrivance was officially announced only to be necessary with the Bakelite IVAs, but it is certain that Mk IVs were also issued complete with these fitments. The thought of wartime raw material shortages cannot have been at the forefront of the designers' minds, for each mask was accompanied by more than two dozen spares and accessories! Although they were widely issued their weight and complexity made them unpopular, and once the Type B helmet became obsolete they were phased out.

The next set of goggles to be introduced was the **Mk VII** announced in AMO N962 of July 1942. The headband was an adjustable, leather-covered, spring-loaded strap, and the heavy, blue-painted brass frames carried split windows. A flip-up anti-glare screen was attached to the nose bridge, and overall they were somewhat smaller than the Mk IVs.

The return to simplicity came with the **Mk VIII** goggles announced in October 1943. Lightweight, of simple construction and adjustment and with a generous and comfortably padded, suede-lined surround, they remained in service for the rest of

1: Flight Lieutenant, RAF, Service Dress, 1941
2: Flight Sergeant, RAF/PAF, Service Dress, 1942
3: Corporal, RAF War Service Dress, 1945

A

1: Corporal, RAF Tropical Service Dress, 1939
2: Air Vice Marshal, RAF Tropical Service Dress, 1939
3: Sergeant, WAAF Tropical Service Dress, 1942

B

1: Leading Aircraftwoman, WAAF Working/Shelter Dress, 1943
2: Matron, Princess Mary's RAF Nursing Service, Working Dress, 1941
3: Section Officer, WAAF Service Dress, 1939-45

C

1: Corporal, RAF Regiment, Service Dress, 1942
2: Leading Aircraftman, RAF Regiment, Denims, 1944
3: Corporal, RAF, Heavy Duty Dress, 1944

D

1: Fighter Pilot, Southern England, 1940
2: Fighter Pilot, Libya, 1942
3: Wireless Operator/Air Gunner, North-West Europe, 1944-45

E

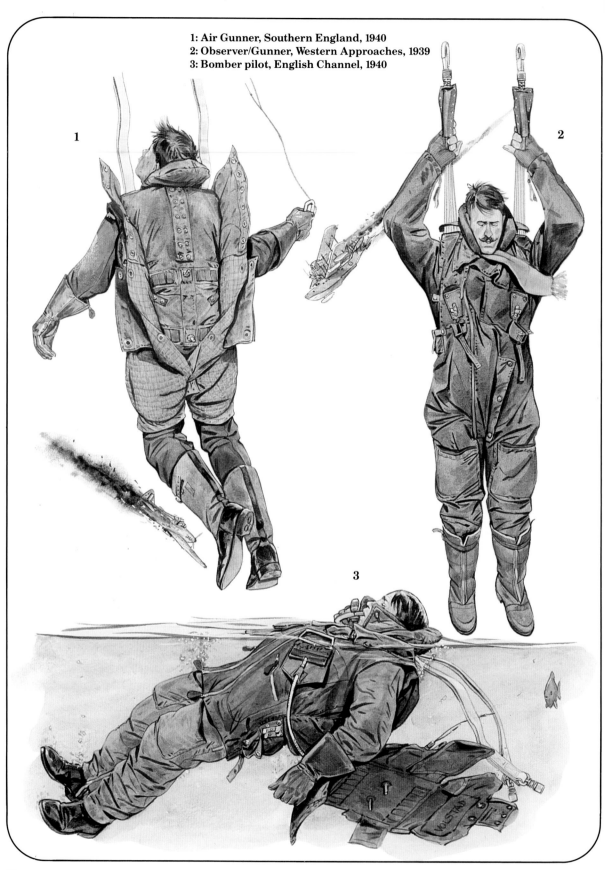

1: Air Gunner, Southern England, 1940
2: Observer/Gunner, Western Approaches, 1939
3: Bomber pilot, English Channel, 1940

F

G

1: Signaller, North Atlantic, 1943
2: Fighter pilot, Burma, 1944
3: Bomber pilot, Malaya, 1945

H

the war, and were not superseded until visors became the means of protecting the aviator's face.

Although a wide range of official pattern goggles was available to aircrews during the war, face protection was obviously a very personal concern. Photographs indicate that privately purchased or captured items were commonly used and that comfort was of far greater importance to the wearer than Air Ministry dictum, so that Mk III and even Mk II goggles continued in use long after they had been officially withdrawn.

In addition to goggles complete leather face masks lined in chamois and suspended from an elastic harness were available. They had apertures for eyes, nostrils and mouth, but as it was impossible to wear them with an oxygen mask they must have been intended for Coastal Command gunners firing through open hatches.

Flying spectacles

The introduction of enclosed cockpit aircraft released Coastal Command observers and aircrew operating in the tropics from the disadvantages of wearing relatively heavy goggles for extended periods of time. They did not, however, overcome the problem of glare encountered when spotting for submarines or when flying over the desert. The Air Ministry introduced spectacles of comfortable, lightweight construction capable of being fitted with tinted lenses. They could also be made to prescription, thereby correcting slight visual accuities permitted among aircrews.

The **Mk V**, **VA** and **VA*** versions announced in June 1940 comprised padded wire frames with clear shatter-proof side pieces and either clear or tinted lenses. They were retained on the helmet by half press-studs on the ends of the arms which engaged with studs fixed to the helmet. The Mk V had a flip-up anti-glare screen and the VA* was equipped with Polaroid lenses.

In the following year the **Mk VB** spectacles were introduced (AMO N1398). They had Polaroid lenses and an adjustable elastic strap suspension system like goggles.

The year 1943 saw the announcement of the **Mk VIII** aircrew spectacles which initiated the trend for a conventional-looking pair of sunglasses. They had steel wire frames but were not issued with correcting lenses. This facility was specifically accorded to aircrews requiring it with the **Mk IX** and **IXA** introduced by AMO A758/44. These spectacles had alternative fixture systems; either ordinary arms or an elastic headband, and the IXs bore clear lenses while the IXAs had tinted ones.

The last wartime variant, the **Mk X**, were only produced with Polaroid lenses and were issued to Coastal Command in place of goggles. They were very similar to the Mk VIII in appearance.

Oxygen masks

The RAF entered the war with the constant-flow oxygen mask **Type D**, which had a green fabric outer and a chamois leather lining. It was attached to the helmet by means of press-studs which engaged with studs on the inside of the face aperture. The form of the mask varied considerably depending upon the microphone with which it was fitted. There were five variants:

Type C Carbon microphone (10A/9004), which was mounted in line with the wearer's nose and had a bell-shaped mic. housing.

Type 19 Electro-Magnetic (10A/10989) contained in a round housing covered, like the Type C, with chamois. Introduced in January 1939.

Type 21 Electro-Magnetic (10A/11994) contained in a large black lacquered circular cover. Introduced in October 1940.

Type 26 Electro-Magnetic (10A/12571) or **Type 28** Carbon (10A/12573), similar to though smaller than the Type 21. Introduced in January 1942.

The Types 26 and 28 required a special rubber adaptor to enable them to fit the mounting ring in the mask. The Type D mask was declared obsolescent in May 1942.

During 1941 the first sophisticated, regulated-flow oxygen mask was introduced under the designation **Type E**. Whereas the Type D had supplied a constant stream of oxygen to the wearer, part of which he breathed in and part of which escaped round the unsealed edges of the mask, the Type E was intended to deliver a more controlled flow, all of which would be used on inhalation. The regulated flow was achieved by use of the Oxygen Economiser Mk I which provided a measured quantity of oxygen, variable according to altitude, to the user during the breathing-in phase of the cycle, and cut off the supply during the breathing-out phase, thus avoiding waste. As it was not necessary to fill the lungs with pure oxygen an inspiratory valve in the mask permitted the lungs to be topped up with air.

The E mask was made of black rubber with a chamois leather skirt which extended beyond the face cup, and had an aluminium plate across the nose which could be bent to achieve a seal round the wearer's face. Its most noticeable feature was a conical trunk into which the oxygen concertina pipe fitted. This trunk housed the dual function inspiratory-expiratory valve, but it was also a condensation trap, and when the accumulated liquid froze at altitude the valve became blocked. The mask also suffered from instability on the face during high-G manoeuvres; it was suspended from the helmet by leather straps attached to bars on the side of the mask. These straps bore press-studs which engaged with similar studs on the outer edges of the helmet face aperture.

A modification to overcome the latter problem was incorporated into the second production batch and consisted of mounting the suspension harness on the wire ring which clamped the microphone, Type 26 or 28, to the mask.

It seems that the major valve problem was not addressed until early 1942—except by 90 Squadron, who made up for themselves a modified mask

The development of the E Type oxygen mask: (1) Type E as issued, spring 1941. (2) Type E Special, modifications incorporated by 90 Squadron, spring/summer 1941. (3) Type E* with new suspension system and inspiratory valve in the left cheek, February 1942.

which can be designated the 'Type E Special'. The unit was operating the first of the B-17 Flying Fortresses and experienced severe icing problems at high altitudes. The modification comprised the removal of the oxygen supply tube and its re-mounting in an angled aluminium inlet pipe in the left cheek, the conversion of the trunk valve to expiratory only, and the addition of an inspiratory valve on the right cheek. As the unit was still wearing B Type helmets various suspension rigs were lashed up to the side bars. On the squadron these modified masks were known unofficially as the 'Type F'.

The development work which had proceeded through 1941 resulted in a substantially modified mask called the **Type E*** which was announced in February 1942. Modification leaflets M48 and M52 of Air Publication 1275 Vol. 2 detail the conversion process, which added an inspiratory valve to the left cheek and a completely new elastic webbing harness, partly attached to the microphone ring, and partly to the trunk. This harness clipped to the left cheek of the C Type helmet and hooked to the right cheek.

Regardless of the modifications effected to the E masks it was evident that further development was required. This must have been proceeding concurrently with the modification to the Es for in August 1942 the **Type G** mask was announced. It was produced in three sizes—large, medium and small—and was fitted with the Type 26 microphone. It was made of grey rubber with an elastic suspension similar to that on the E*. Face sealing

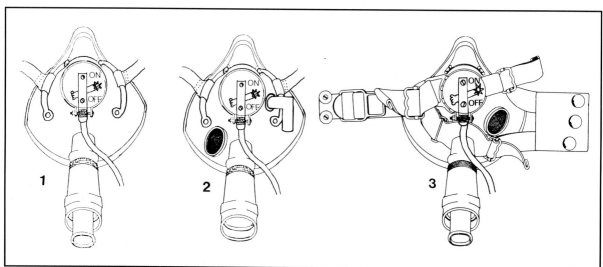

was achieved by means of a copper wire held in loops around the nose section, and the expiratory valve and oxygen inlet pipe shared the lower and upper portions of an oval extension below the microphone. The oxygen outlets on the inside wall of the face cup were well above the level at which condensation could accumulate, thereby avoiding the freezing problem. The attached wiring for intercom was minimal due to the introduction of the C Type wired helmet.

This mask gradually came to be used by all aircrews and was not replaced until after the war.

Portable oxygen

When working away from crew stations at altitudes above 10,000 feet it was necessary to use oxygen from small cylinders which gave about ten minutes supply. The original method of carriage was a grey tubular canvas pouch on shoulder and waist straps worn under the parachute harness. Later the cylinders were fitted with a hook which slid on to the parachute harness. The bayonet connector from the D Type mask fitted directly onto the cylinder outlet, but the E and G masks required extension tubes and adaptors to take their large bore concertina pipes. Oxygen cylinders were always painted black.

Suits, Aircrew

Service Dress uniform was not well adapted for wear under flying clothing and AMO A909 of December 1940 announced more convenient garments for flying personnel. The suits were in fact a blue-grey version of Army Battledress comprising a short jacket with breast pockets, shoulder straps and an integral belt, accompanied by trousers with buttoned ankle tabs to assist the donning of flying boots. All button fastenings were concealed by flies, and the trousers bore a flapped pocket on the left thigh and a Field Service Dressing pocket on the upper right front as well as ordinary side pockets. Officers wore rank lace on the shoulder straps, but warrant officers and NCOs wore rank badges on the right sleeve only. The latter also wore shoulder eagles.

In 1943 Suits, Aircrew were transformed from flying clothing into uniform under the title War Service Dress, and lost the trouser tabs and both special pockets.

Flying suits

Since the latter days of World War I the one-piece overall had been the most popular form of flying dress. The **Patterns 1930** and **1940** were identical in shape, the former being made of thin, proofed khaki cotton, the latter of thick, pale drab gaberdine. Both were worn with detachable brown fleece collars and with liners of fur fabric (22C/53) or quilted kapok (22C/102). In December 1942 an electrically wired version of the '40 Pattern was introduced, as well as a new suit known as the **'Buoyant Type' or Taylor Suit**. This garment was yellow in colour and was fitted with full-length leg zips to aid dressing. It was electrically wired for use with D Type Electrically Heated inner gloves and socks, though some examples were produced for use with RAE EH outer gloves and boots (see section on electrically heated clothing). The whole suit was heavily padded with kapok, and had pockets in the chest, legs and behind the head for extra buoyancy pads. A torch pocket appeared on the right and a fluorescine pack on the left, as on the Mk I life jacket.

The most well-known flying suit of the war was the **Irvin** two-piece suit made of brown sheepskin. Introduced in 1938, it was produced the following year in a wired version for RAE type accessories, and later with a special bright yellow hood for Coastal Command.

Combined pattern flying suits

The bulk of normal flying clothing was often a problem in the cramped interiors of 1930s-designed aircraft, and garments were therefore devised which incorporated the functions of several different pieces of kit in one.

The **Flying Suit, Combined Pattern** introduced in October 1939 was intended for Coastal Command crews, and comprised a silk cord parachute harness sewn onto a jerkin which buttoned inside a BG outer suit. Sandwiched between the two was a gas-operated life jacket bladder. The suit was made in four variants for wear in aircraft with enclosed or open cockpits/gun positions, the former covering the torso only, the latter being full overalls. The harness was produced in three variants for use with seat or chest type parachute packs or a choice of either. In all cases the lift webs emerged from the shoulders of the suit within

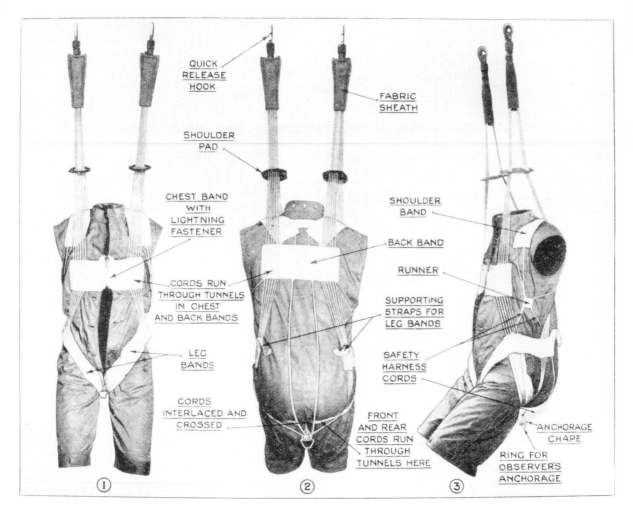

The inner jerkin of the Flying Suit, Combined Pattern showing the disposition of the silk cord parachute harness. (**Air Publication 1275 Vol. I**)

sleeves which were tacked with breaking stitches to the chest and/or back. The webs ended in special snap hooks which clipped to the parachute D-rings. On landing in water the parachutist discarded his canopy by pulling collars on the hooks which, by means of springs, released the hook part complete with canopy from the element attached to the lift webs.

The **Irvin Harnessuit** announced in May 1940 was provided for Bomber and Coastal Commands and certain fighter units. It was a short-legged jerkin incorporating a life jacket bladder and a webbing parachute harness with the special quick release snap hooks. Like the Combined Pattern Flying Suit it could be used with seat or chest type packs; but its lift webs were retained in press-stud-fastened flaps on the chest and back

which pulled open when the parachute canopy deployed. When a seat pack was used a flap housing the rip cord handle was attached to the lower left side by means of a loop and hook, a turn-stud and a 'lift the dot' fastener. An identical arrangement was used on the FS, Combined Pattern.

The **GQ Parasuit** was supplied exclusively to gunners of Boulton Paul Defiant aircraft. It took the form of a smock incorporating a webbing harness very similar in appearance to the Harnessuit at the front, but having at the back two large flaps within which a parachute canopy was housed; a smaller pair of leather-covered flaps retained a spring-form drogue parachute. On pulling the rip cord the small flaps were forced open by the drogue, which initiated the deployment of the main chute, whose exit burst the zip or press-stud fastening of the upper flap section, thus permitting the lift webs to emerge at the shoulders.

As with the other suits a life jacket stole was provided in the chest compartment, and quick release links joined the canopy to the lift webs.

Electrically heated clothing

Electrically heated flying clothing had been available to aviators from the latter days of World War I. Between the wars it was sparingly issued in the RAF, predominantly to Meteorological Unit personnel who were required to fly at very high altitudes. The change in Bomber Command's tactics, the necessity to fly all year round and the greater heights at which operations were conducted subjected aircrews to a range of temperatures which could vary from minus 18° at 20,000 feet in July to minus 45° at 27,000 feet in February. In these circumstances crew efficiency could only be maintained by the provision of some type of heating, whether ambient or personal.

Two variants of EH clothing were used. The older form was known as the **Royal Aircraft Establishment** type and was characterised by two-pin Bakelite plugs. It was most commonly seen incorporated into the Irvin flying suit, for which it provided heat to special ankle boots and outer gloves. If body heating was required a blue-grey inner waistcoat was worn to which the gloves and, by means of connectors, the boots were linked. This arrangement could be worn under non-wired Irvin suits or any of the overall type flying suits. Both the wired Irvin suit and the EH waistcoat had a permanently attached in-put lead which emerged from the right rear hem. Gloves and boots were attached to the other clothing by means of 'pull the dot' fasteners so that the wearer's movement did not disconnect the plugs.

In January 1942 (AMO N134) **Electrically Heated Clothing Type D** was announced. This set was specifically designed for use with the wired 1941 Pattern suit and the Taylor suit. All of its electrical connections were achieved by means of press-stud terminals and its gloves and socks were worn inside ordinary gauntlets or boots. The amount of heating could be varied by wearing or discarding certain components of the set, so that hands and feet could be catered for by clipping gloves and socks to the outer suit; torso heat could be provided by adding a waistcoat, or all-over heat by a full length liner which buttoned inside the '41 or Taylor suits. The body and extremity electrical circuits were linked by multi-terminal pads which connected the lining to the outer suit, and power in-put was fed through a belt pad which fastened inside the suit over the right kidney, the wire passing through slits in the clothing to the aircraft electrical system.

It appears that certain '41 Pattern EW suits were produced which had both press-stud and RAE terminals so that either type of glove or boot/sock could be worn. In addition it was possible to mix and match RAE and D Type boots, socks, inner and outer gloves by means of adaptors incorporating both types of terminals (AMO A1360/42).

An improved higher wattage version of the Type D clothing had been issued by 1944, and was designated **Type G**. Visually there was no difference between the two sets, but Ds bore stores references 22c 714-719 and Gs 22c 896-901 (AMO N295/44).

By winter 1943 it was usually only the air gunners who required this sort of kit; cockpit heating being adequate for the rest of the crew. Some fighter pilots probably also wore EH waist-

Flt. Lt. F. C. A. Lanning, DFC, 141 Squadron, wearing the GQ Parasuit with Irvin jacket and '39 Pattern boots. (Courtesy Lanning/Chambers)

coats, particularly those engaged in high altitude, long range photo-reconnaissance and met flights.

Gloves and gauntlets

Accurate flying and manipulation of weapons demands warm hands, and at the beginning of the war the RAF had a handwear package which consisted of silk and chamois inner gloves with woollen fingerless mitts and brown leather outer gauntlets. The **1933 Pattern** gauntlet with vertical cuff zips was superseded in 1941 by a similar item with diagonal zips, and in 1943 by a loose fitting gauntlet with no fasteners at all. This item seems principally to have been designed to ease the wearing of bulky electrically heated inner gloves; however, smaller sizes of it were introduced by AMO N295/44 for wear with thinner non-heated inners.

The oddity among the RAF's gauntlets was the **1940 Pattern**, which was specifically designed for use with chemical heating pads. As an interim measure until electrical heating became widely available an American medical apparatus was adopted, in the form of a sachet containing a 'chemical cocktail' which when dampened produced heat for up to six hours. The gauntlets were made of heavily greased cream sheepskin with brown leather thumbs and finger gussets. The heating sachet was contained in a small pocket positioned on the back of the hand. The efficiency of the method depended on adding only a very small amount of water to the sachet; too much produced chemical burns. This unreliability and their great bulk made them unpopular. 'Bags Everhot', as the sachets were called, could also be used inside '40 and '41 Pattern flying boots.

By 1945 cockpit heating permitted the introduction of thin cape leather gloves with excellent tactile properties. Their use was confined to temperate climates, however, as they became very stiff if subjected to sweat.

A Whitley crew wearing 1930 Pattern and Irvin flying suits with, far right, an Irvin Harnessuit, Observer Type. Note the variety of gloves and gauntlets. (RAFM CEB 173/10)

Flying boots

From the earliest days of flying it had been recognised that the feet needed special protection from the cold. By 1939 the thigh length 'fug' boots beloved of First World War aviators had disappeared, though they remained an issue item for several years after the introduction of the **1930 Pattern** boot. These latter were made of chestnut suede lined in sheepskin and incorporated an extensive rubber galosh round the foot. They had a front zip fastening and a tightening strap at the top. Although they had been superseded by the **1936 Pattern** and indeed the 1939 Pattern before the beginning of the war, some still remained in use.

The **1936 Pattern** was the most elegant flying boot of the war and was popular enough to continue in use long after other versions were issued. It was a straight, pull-on, black leather, fleece-lined boot with a short tightening strap at the top. Its replacement, the **1939 Pattern**, was an unsatisfactory product featuring the foot of the '36 with a vulcanised fabric leg which, despite treatment, did not repel the dew from long runway grass and in consequence froze at altitude.

Both the 1936 and 1939 Patterns were too tight about the leg for flying suits to be comfortably tucked into them. July 1941 therefore saw the introduction of a new boot which was very similar to the old '30 Pattern. It was produced from brown split hide with sheepskin lining, a front zip, composition sole, and a small rubber galosh to make it waterproof. The zip closure permitted legwear to be tucked in. This type was officially designated **1940 Pattern** despite its introduction date (22C 435—442). Operational experience soon proved, however, that the tuck-in provision had so loosened the legs of the boots that on baling out they were often sucked off by the slipstream. A minor modification was incorporated to prevent this in the form of a tan leather ankle strap, but no matter how minor this was it prompted the Air Ministry to redesignate the boots as **1941 Pattern** with the new stores code 22C 748—755.

Baling out and the associated problems of evading capture in enemy-occupied Europe gave rise to the final model of flying boots designed during the war. In the course of 1942 some of the squadrons undertaking fighter sweeps over France

Basic though characteristic flying kit is worn by these two Hurricane pilots: '36 boots, '32 life jackets with B Type helmets and D Variant 2 oxygen masks. The left figure wears Mk IV goggles while his comrade sports the obsolete Mk IIs. (RAFM CEB 213/16A)

were issued with a prototype boot consisting of a black leather shoe with a detachable leather leg; the shoe laced up and the leg zipped, either at the front or slightly to the outer side. A short tab and buckle was provided for tightening, and the lining of both parts was the usual sheepskin. These trials were evidently successful for this boot, slightly modified with a suede leg, was introduced as the **Escape type, 1943 Pattern**, though no AMO has been found to pinpoint the date.

All flying boots had multi-layered, splinterproof interlinings.

Life jackets

One of the most characteristic features of RAF flying kit during the first two years of the war was the old **1932 Pattern** life jacket. It was a thick, khaki cotton twill waistcoat closing with three buttons and two buckled straps and housing an orally inflated bladder, the inflation tube for which emerged from the left lapel. The front section of the garment was often painted yellow to make the wearer more visible when down in the sea.

39

A motley collection of kit worn by Gladiator pilots of 112 Squadron, Egypt, 1940. Note the instructions printed on the 1932 Ptn life jackets. (RAFM PC 72/89/91)

In July 1941 the **Life Jacket Mk I** was introduced (AMO N811), and remained in service with modifications for the rest of the war. It was dull yellow in colour, similar in cut to the '32 Pattern, but the bladder was filled from a break-neck carbon dioxide cylinder located on the lower right side; the oral inflation tube was still provided for topping up. On the lower rear left side a fluorescine sea marker pack was attached; and a floating flap extending from behind the head was supposed to make the wearer more visible to rescue aircraft.

Throughout 1942 modifications were incorporated into the garment: handles on the chest and leg tapes to make it easier to haul a helpless wearer from the water (AMO N88); a pocket for a whistle, another for a yellow skull cap, and D-rings for the attachment of the K Type dinghy pack (AMO N509); and in the following year a torch pocket on the right rear side and a life line on the left for connection to the dinghy (AMO N760 & 1370). The floating flap and the skull cap were with-drawn when dinghies became commonly available, but a heliograph mirror was added in the left breast pocket for attracting attention.

Life jackets were sometimes decorated with painted mottos, talismans, cartoons or simply the wearer's name.

Parachutes and dinghies

It was not until 1925 that aircraft parachutes were compulsorily worn in the RAF despite the fact that practical models had existed during the First World War; balloon observers had been equipped with them since 1917.

For operational purposes there were two main forms usually designated according to the location in which they were worn—hence chest and seat types. The latter tended to be the preserve of pilots only, though some captains of large bombers preferred to wear chest types like the rest of their crew. Only rarely did Coastal Command crews bother with parachutes, as the low altitude of most of their operations would not have given enough time for the apparatus to function properly, and in any case survival chances were improved by staying with the aircraft and ditching.

The harness of both types consisted of double thickness white cotton and linen mixture webbing sewn together and provided with white metal adjustment and attachment fittings. Connecting to the Quick Release Box mounted over the abdomen, two straps passed over the shoulders and another pair round the upper legs, through an inter-leg loop and then to the QR Box. The latter was positioned on a broad strop on the wearer's left side, which on seat types also accommodated the rip cord handle. The wire cord itself passed through a wire gauze tube attached to the broad strop and the pack. Seat packs were permanently fixed to the harness and the lift webs were inter-linked to the shoulder straps.

Chest harnesses were constructed in the same way, but had no broad strop; the lift webs fell forwards over the chest terminating in snap hooks which were retained in fittings attached to plates of webbing sewn just above the QR Box connectors. The chest pack had two protruding D-rings at the back to engage with the snap hooks, and a rip cord handle on the front.

Both assemblies were provided with back pads which were attached to the harness by means of tabs and press-studs. The seat type also had a cushion through which the inter-leg loop emerged. All aircrew canopies were white—silk until 1943, thereafter gradually replaced with nylon.

Although dinghies, housed within the wing cavity, were provided for ditching in the larger aircraft, it was impossible so to accommodate them in the smaller aircraft. Until 1942 fighter pilots had to rely on their life jackets, which would certainly keep them afloat and with their head out of water; but against this must be reckoned the fact that, at least in winter, they would die of exposure within about 75 minutes. From January of that year survival chances were somewhat improved by the introduction of the **K Type one man dinghy** (AMO N5).

Housed in a rectangular parcel which included the carbon dioxide inflation cylinder, the pack could be connected to the parachute harness in place of the seat cushion or, on a chest type, as an additional cushion. Back packs were also produced to replace the back pad. Dinghy packs were always provided with a webbing lanyard which was attached to the life jacket so that on discarding his parachute harness the airman retained the dinghy pack.

* * *

Conclusion

Despite rationing and the uncertainties of raw materials supply it was never the case that the RAF in the United Kingdom suffered a shortage of uniform or flying clothing. That fact should not, however, lead the researcher to imagine that the

Wellington crew, Mildenhall, autumn 1941. The air gunners at far right and centre wear Electrically Wired Irvin suits with RAE Type ankle boots. (RAFM/Mildenhall Albums)

Typhoon pilots of 198 Squadron, Normandy, 1944. Life jackets are worn with C/G helmet/mask combinations and '43 boots over War Service Dress. (RAFM DB 61)

clothing supplied was always worn in the manner intended by the Air Ministry. There are various orders which remind the force of the clothing regulations, and there are well-documented instances of oddities: radar mechanics colouring the centre flash of the wireless operators' arm badge with red ink, unofficial shoulder titles, WAAFs wearing FS caps in the UK, metal squadron insignia being worn on uniform (8 and 213 Squadrons), etc. A very detailed study of photographs will occasionally reveal unfamiliar or anomalous usages particularly in the flying clothing field: e.g. kapok-quilted flying suit liners or Type D Electrically Heated clothing being worn as outer garments, or an electrically heated air gunner's hand muff!

Whilst not pretending to be a comprehensive study of the subject it is hoped that this book will, at least, enable the uniform and flying clothing researcher to recognise what he sees and to group together the kit in appropriate period ensembles.

Bibliography

Air Ministry Orders Series A and N 1938–1945

Air Publications

AP 1275 Vols 1 & 2 Instrument Manual (Oxygen Equipment)

AP 1182 Vols 1 & 2 Parachute Manual (Parachutes, Dinghies, Combined Pattern Flying Suits)

AP 1186 Vol 1 Signals Manual (Microphones and Earphones)

AP 1095A Vol 1 Electrical Equipment Manual (Electrically Heated Clothing)

AP 1385 1st Edition Dress Regulations for Officers

The Plates

A1: Flight Lieutenant, RAF, Service Dress, 1941
Wearing the standard officers' Service Dress with gas mask case and helmet this Czech officer prepares to go on leave. He is distinguished by nationality titles and the Czech pilot's badge worn on the right breast pocket. AMO A555/40 specified the positions of country of origin titles as being

the shoulders of jackets and greatcoats and the wrists of raincoats. Our figure also wears the ribbon of the Distinguished Flying Cross.

A2: Flight Sergeant, RAF/PAF, Service Dress, 1942
In 1941 the Poles negotiated a new agreement with HMG which placed their Air Force on a more independent footing than formerly, though still within the RAF. This Air Gunner wears PAF badges alongside his RAF insignia, and the red and white cord on his collar rank badges indicates that he is a cadet-under-training at the Officer Cadet Training Unit. AMO A44/41 laid down that firearms were to be carried by personnel in transit to courses of instruction.

A3: Corporal, RAF, War Service Dress, 1945
Although there had been an Air-Sea Rescue Service from very early in the war its distinctive

badge was not introduced until 1943 (AMO A17). Our Wireless Operator/Mechanic wears WSD with the new beret and its black plastic badge.

B1: Corporal, RAF Tropical Service Dress, 1939
The Pith Hat was worn in India after 1938 in preference to the Wolseley helmet which was retained for Middle East use. With that difference alone this Physical Training Instructor could be serving anywhere between Gibraltar and Singapore. He wears the old drab 1908 Pattern webbing equipment; and note General Service Medal.

B2: Air Vice Marshal, RAF Tropical Service Dress, 1939
The officers' jacket differed from the airmen's only in having pointed cuffs, shoulder boards and buttoned skirt pockets. Within a year, and for less formal occasions, the air officers' FS cap piped in pale blue would replace the round cap.

B3: Sergeant, WAAF Tropical Service Dress, 1942
Some WAAF NCO instructors served in the Middle East from late 1941. Over her practical, if inelegant bush jacket this sergeant carries the water bottle and haversack required when in operational areas; they are both drawn from the 1925 Pattern set.

C1: Leading Aircraftwoman, WAAF Working/Shelter Dress, 1943
The dark blue slacks issued for Working Dress were very generously cut, and were normally worn with a long cotton dust coat of the same colour for indoor duty. Even when worn with the SD jacket they were restricted to 'on station' use only; skirts were mandatory for all formal parades and for any public appearances outside the station.

C2: Matron, Princess Mary's RAF Nursing Service, Working Dress, 1941
The winter coat-frock with maroon and pale blue lace is here worn with the 1936 Pattern cloak with its status-colour collar and lining; note also the medical badges on the collar. The storm cap had

Sgt. 'Titch' Newman in the 1930 Ptn. flying suit with '39 boots. He carries a D Type mask with separate wiring loom fitted with microphone and telephones. (Courtesy C. Leach, Esq.)

43

blue-grey fabric turned-up false peaks at front and rear, the former bearing the standard officer's cap badge. It was sometimes worn in the wards as well, certainly in field hospitals, and with Suits, Working Serge when the PMs adopted that dress in 1944.

C3: Section Officer, WAAF Service Dress, 1939–45

Whilst their airwomen had a wide range of working clothing WAAF officers had only SD until the middle of the war. This reflected the Air Ministry's perception of them as supervisors and administrators and their status as 'ladies'. As the success of women in the services came to be recognised the old preconceptions evaporated, and a greater practicality of dress was permitted.

The crew of Lancaster W4842, 106 Squadron, operational between December 1942 and May 1943, when the aircraft was lost in action. The two gunners carry electrically heated kit, Type D; B and C Type helmets are in use with E* and G masks; and '36, '39 and '40 Pattern boots can be distinguished. (RAFM DB 48)

D1: Corporal, RAF Regiment, Service Dress, 1942

Based on a photograph of a parade in London being inspected by Maj. Gen. Liardet, the Regiment's first Inspector General, this figure shows the compromises in colour and positioning which had to be made when wearing active service drab webbing and the gas mask haversack with Service Dress. This corporal could be a signaller like his colleague D2, but the crossed flags and thunderbolt badge was only worn on khaki kit (AMO A207/44).

D2: Leading Aircraftman, RAF Regiment, Denims, 1944

Thick cotton denims were issued to the Regiment for exercises and operations, and printed badges were always worn on them instead of embroidered ones. This signaller is heavily laden with a Sten gun Mk. II and a No. 18 radio set; signallers' armament was at the discretion of squadron commanders and some wore only pistol equipment. Apart from rifle squadrons the Regiment

included armoured car and anti-aircraft units for reconnaissance and airfield defence.

D3: Corporal, RAF, Heavy Duty Dress, 1944
Pictured aboard HMS *Largs*, a Landing Ship HQ (Large) which operated as an advanced Operations Room and communications centre between the Normandy invasion fleet and No. 11 Group Fighter Command HQ outside London, this plotter wears the Army khaki Battle Dress used by many front-line branches of the RAF. He has privately purchased the embroidered version of the Combined Operations badge which he wears in preference to the duller official printed issue, and he wears it in the position favoured by Naval personnel; land-based RAF personnel wore it in the Army style on the upper sleeves.

E1: Fighter pilot, Southern England, 1940
This flight lieutenant of 501 (County of Warwick) Squadron scrambles for his Hurricane wearing the white cotton twill overalls which were very popular in the early war years. Certain squadrons used black overalls, and by no means all wore unit badges. Our pilot has painted the front of his 1932 Pattern life jacket yellow to increase his chances of being spotted in case of ditching, but otherwise his kit—B helmet, Mk. IV goggles, D mask and '36 Pattern boots—is standard.

E2: Fighter pilot, Libya, 1942
Sartorial elegance took a knock in the desert and this Kittihawk pilot wears a combination of khaki drill and blue-grey kit under a Heavy Duty Dress blouse. He has been issued with an E/D mask/helmet set which he wears with Mk. VA flying spectacles, chamois leather gloves and '41 Pattern boots. His Mk. I life jacket is the old 'flap' type with kapok-stuffed edges to make it float, and is adorned with a personal mascot.

E3: Wireless Operator/Air Gunner, North-West Europe, 1944–45
Based on a photograph of Flt. Sgt. Frank Nutkins of 180 Squadron (flying B25 Mitchells); we see that the bulky early-war clothing has been largely dispensed with. He wears the later blue aircrew sweater under War Service Dress, 1941 Pattern gauntlets and '43 Pattern 'escape boots'. For

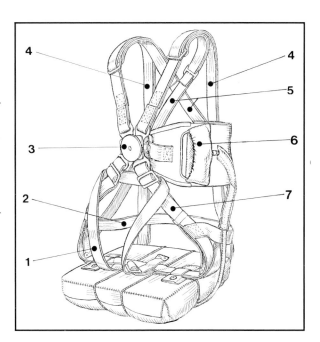

Seat Type parachute without cushion or back pad: (1) Inter-leg loop. (2) Back support strap. (3) Quick release box. (4) Lift webs. (5) Shoulder straps. (6) Rip cord handle housing. (7) Upper leg strap (left). (Air Publication 1275 Vol. 1)

comfort's sake he has fastened only the shoulder straps of his parachute harness; the leg straps will be done up in the aircraft.

F1: Air Gunner, Southern England, 1940
Caught a few seconds after evacuating his Boulton Paul Defiant, this unusually lucky gunner is posed to allow us to see the internal workings of his GQ Parasuit as his canopy deploys above him. Note the loops which retain the parachute cords, and the pierced studs which hold the large and small flaps together when the rip cord pins are in place.

F2: Observer/Gunner, Western Approaches, 1939
Suspended from his chest pack parachute, this Stranraer crewman wears the full-length Flying Suit, Combined Pattern used in aircraft with open gun positions. Note the silk cord harness emerging from the shoulders, the life jacket bladder inflation lever housing on the right side, and the old 1930 Pattern boots. He sports his RAF College First Fifteen Rugby scarf.

F3: Bomber pilot, English Channel, 1940
Shot down on a leaflet raid over Europe, this Whitley pilot tops up the internally housed life

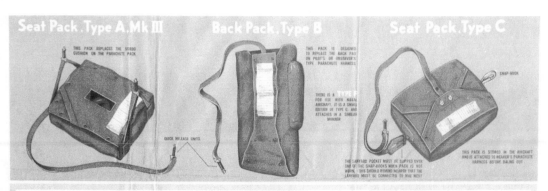

Seat Pack. Type A. Mk III

THIS PACK REPLACES THE SEAT
CUSHION ON THE PARACHUTE PACK

QUICK RELEASE UNITS

Back Pack. Type B

THIS PACK IS DESIGNED
TO REPLACE THE BACK PAD
ON PILOT'S OR OBSERVER'S
TYPE PARACHUTE HARNESS

THERE IS A LARGER
FOR USE WITH NAVAL
AIRCRAFT. IT IS A SMALL
EDITION OF TYPE C AND
ATTACHES IN A SIMILAR
MANNER

THE LANYARD POCKET MUST BE SLIPPED OVER
ONE OF THE SNAP-HOOKS WHEN PACK IS NOT
WORN. THIS SHOULD REMIND WEARER THAT THE
LANYARD MUST BE CONNECTED TO MAE WEST

Seat Pack. Type C

SNAP-HOOK

THIS PACK IS STOWED IN THE AIRCRAFT
IS ATTACHED TO WEARER'S PARACHUTE
HARNESS BEFORE BALING OUT

Type A. Mk III

QUICK RELEASE UNIT WHICH
ATTACHES TO LOOP ON MAE WEST

WEARER ATTACHMENT LANYARD

OXYGEN
BOTTLE
CONTAINER

BASE

COMPASS COVER

LEAK STOPPERS

QUICK RELEASE UNIT

SAIL AND
MAST

DINGHY
ATTACHMENT
PAINTER

THWART AND HELIOGRAPH
STOWAGES ON UNDERSIDE
OF COVER

Type B

COVER

DETACHABLE
RELEASE FLAP

WEARER
ATTACHMENT
LANYARD

QUICK RELEASE UNIT

SAIL AND
MAST

THWART PADDLES

DINGHY ATTACHMENT PAINTER

Type C

WEARER
ATTACHMENT LANYARD

DETACHABLE FLAP AND FALSE
BOTTOM WHICH CONTAINS
THE STOWED ACCESSORIES

SNAP-HOOK
COVERED BY
LANYARD POCKET

QUICK RELEASE
UNIT

LEAK
STOPPERS

SAIL AND
MAST

BASE

SNAP-HOOK

THWART AND HELIOGRAPH
STOWAGES ON UNDERSIDE
OF COVER

DINGHY ATTACHMENT PAINTER

RTP

K-DINGHY - *Fitting*

Printed for H.M. Stationery Office by Wm. Brown & Co. Ltd. London E.C.1.—SC.695.

AIR DIAGRAM 3980	AMENDMENTS AND DETAILS DATE		PREPARED BY MINISTRY OF AIRCRAFT PRODUCTION FOR PROMULGATION BY
LAT 1 OF SHEETS 3			AIR MINISTRY
SEPT 1943			

46

jacket bladder of his Irvin Harnessuit. He has released his canopy from the quick release hooks whose stubs remain on the lift webs; but he has yet to discard the pack of his seat-type parachute which hangs from the rip cord housing clipped to his side. Note that it was standard practice to take off both helmet and oxygen mask before baling out of an aircraft.

G1: Air Gunner, East Anglia, 1941
At a bomber station in eastern England this Wellington gunner slips a 'Bag Everhot' into his Chemically Heated Gauntlets Pattern 1940; he already has a pair of these heat pads tucked into each of his boots. His chest-type parachute harness and pack lie ready to be donned over his Life Jacket, Flap Type; and he already wears the container for his Portable Oxygen Mk. I. On his helmet we see the attachment plates for a pair of Goggles Mk. IVA, though he has dispensed with the goggles themselves. His oxygen is supplied through a Mask Type D Variant 3.

G2: Air Gunner, East Anglia, 1942
The first widely issued electrically heated clothing was designated Type D and was worn as the fourth layer over rayon underwear, the white Aircrew Frock/Sweater and the Suit, Aircrew. As a fifth layer the crewman could wear a kapok-filled liner, and finally either an Irvin Suit, a Flying Suit Pattern 1930 or 1940, an Electrically Wired Suit Pattern 1941, or a Taylor Suit—plus, of course, his Mae West and parachute harness. Note the slipper-like 'socks' and their T-bar connectors fastening up to the waistcoat; also the power supply lead and its connector pad on the right side.

G3: Air Gunner, East Anglia, 1944
Having struggled into his Taylor Buoyancy Suit with G Type electrical heating, this Lancaster gunner heads for the lorry to take him out to his aircraft. The EH glove connectors can be clearly seen at the wrists but the only other indication of heating is the power supply lead. His Mk. II

Portable Oxygen is shown hooked up, though in reality he would not take a cylinder until he was inside the aircraft. As no life jacket was required with the Taylor Suit the high visibility colour of the Mae West has been used for the entire suit.

H1: Signaller, North Atlantic, 1943
For the crews of Sunderland flying boats airborne for perhaps 14 hours on convoy escort or anti-submarine patrols, flying clothing had to be comfortable enough to be really lived in. Many crews preferred to wear head-sets rather than the constricting helmets; and as maritime operations were conducted at low altitudes parachute harnesses and hot, sweaty oxygen masks were superfluous. In case of ditching it was a good idea to have a high visibility hood to supplement the yellow Mae West. Our signaller carries an Aldis Morse lamp for flashing messages to shipping.

H2: Fighter pilot, Burma, 1944
Despite the dangers from cockpit fire of flying with exposed flesh the heat of Burma has proved too much for this Spitfire pilot. Shorts and a bush jacket make up his flying kit, along with the Type E helmet in Aertex material, a G mask and Mk. VIII Anti-Glare Spectacles. He has replaced his flying boots with suede 'mosquito' boots, and he carries a machette, a waterbottle and a revolver in case of having to bale out.

H3: Bomber pilot, Malaya, 1945
The only specially designed aviation kit for Far East wear was this combined flying/evasion suit which was issued in spring 1945. Made of thin cotton, it included a hessian and leather belt for weapons and attachment points in the chest for a pack containing evasion/survival aids. A peaked cap with red flannel lining and a mosquito net to combat ultra-violet sunlight and insects respectively was a standard accessory. This Liberator captain has taken the wise precaution of flying in marching boots and puttees.

The K Type Dinghy Pack variants, Air Diagram 3980. Note the rectangular aperture in the Type A Mk III to allow the passage of the inter-leg loop from the parachute harness. (Crown copyright, by permission of the Controller of HMSO)

Notes sur les planches en couleur

A1 La tenue standard de service pour les officiers avec étui de masque à gaz et casque, titres de nationalité les distinguant, écusson de pilote tchèque sur la poche du côté gauche de la poitrine et ruban de la Distinguished Flying Cross. **A2** Ecussons de la Force aérienne polonaise portés à côté de l'insigne de la RAF; la ganse rouge et blanche sur les insignes de grade du col indique qu'il s'agit d'un élève officier (cadet-under-training) de l'Unité d'Instruction des élèves officiers. **A3** Tenue de service pendant la guerre avec le nouveau béret et son insigne de plastique noir. L'insigne du Service de Sauvetage aérien en mer n'a été introduit qu'en 1943.

B1 Ancien modèle d'équipement en toile grise olivâtre de 1908 et chapeau en sola; notez la médaille de 'General Service'. **B2** Veste d'officier à parements à pointe, pattes d'épaule et poches boutonnées de la jupe. Il ne fallut qu'une seule année pour que la casquette ronde soit remplacée par le calot des Officiers de l'Air. **B3** Ce sergent porte le bidon et la musette modèle de 1925 sur sa saharienne.

C1 Pantalons bleus foncés distribués comme tenue de travail, portés généralement avec un long manteau de coton de même couleur, contre la poussière, pour les tâches en intérieur. **C2** Redingote d'hiver avec ganse marron et bleue pâle portée avec le manteau, modèle de 1936, dont la couleur du col et de la doublure indique le rang; notez également les insignes du corps médical sur le col. La casquette contre les intempéries avait de fausses visières retroussées à l'avant et à l'arrière, la première portant l'insigne de coiffure standard de l'officier. **C3** Les officiers de la WAAF n'eurent qu'une tenue de service (Service Dress) jusqu'au milieu de la guerre.

D1 Tenue de service portée avec le webbing gris olivâtre du service des Archives et la musette de masque à gaz. **D2** Epais treillis en coton avec insignes imprimés. Il porte un Sten Gun Mk II et un poste radio N° 18. **D3** Tenue de combat kaki de l'armée utilisée par plusieurs services du front de la RAF avec version brodée de l'insigne des Opérations interarmes porté à l'emplacement préféré du personnel naval.

E1 Treillis blancs de croisé en coton qui furent populaires pendant les premières années de guerre. Le devant du gilet de sauvetage, modèle 1932, a été peint en jaune, il porte un casque B, des lunettes de protection Mk IV, un masque D et des bottes modèle 36. **E2** Un mélange de tenue d'exercice kaki et de kit bleu-gris sous un blouson. Il a un casque/masque D/E avec des lunettes de vol Mk. VA, des gants en peau de chamois et des bottes modèle 41. Le gilet de sauvetage Mk. I est l'ancien style 'flap'. **E3** Le pull-over bleu des équipages aériens plus récent porté sous la tenue de Service de Guerre, gantelets modèle 1941 et bottes 'escape'.

F1 Intérieur d'une combinaison GQ de para. **F2** Combinaison complète de vol, modèle mixte utilisé dans les appareils dont les positions des canons sont découvertes, et modèle 1930 de bottes. **F3** La combinaison à harnais Irvin avec vessie de gilet de sauvetage logée à l'intérieur.

G1 Ce canonnier a un 'Bag Everhot' glissé dans chacune de ses bottes et dans ses Gantelets chauffés chimiquement, modèle 1940. Il a également un parachute de type fixé à la poitrine, une veste de sauvetage, de type 'flap', le conteneur pour son masque à oxygène portatif Mk. 1 et un Masque Type D variation 3. **G2** Vêtements de type D chauffés électriquement et portés sur les sous-vêtements en rayonne, la tunique blanche, le pull-over de petite tenue et la combinaison, pour équipage. **G3** Une combinaison 'Taylor Bouyancy' avec chauffage électrique, type G, en couleur de haute visibilité et masque à oxygène agrafé portatif Mk II.

H1 De nombreux équipages d'hydravion portaient lors des patrouilles longues des casques radio plutôt que les casques courants et retiraient leurs harnais de parachute et masques à oxygène. Le masque de haute visibilité venait s'ajouter au Mae West. **H2** Le kit de vol comprenait des shorts et une saharienne avec le casque de type E Aertex, un masque G et des lunettes anti-éblouissantes Mk-VIII. Il porte des bottes en peau de chamois 'Mosquito' et une machette, un bidon et un revolver. **H3** Combinaison d'évasion/de vol conçue pour l'Extrême-Orient et distribuée au printemps 1945. Faite en coton, elle comprend un ceinturon en cuir et toile de chanvre pour les armes. Une casquette à visière avec doublure en flanelle rouge et une moustiquaire étaient également courantes.

Farbtafeln

A1 Die standardmäßige Dienstuniform eines Offiziers mit Gasmaskenbehältnis und Helm, der sich durch Nationalitätsabzeichen unterscheidet. Das tschechische Pilotenabzeichen auf der rechten Brusttasche und das Band der Flugkreuzauszeichnung. **A2** Die Abzeichen der polnischen Luftwaffe wurden neben denen der RAF getragen. Die rote und weiße Kordel am Kragenrangabzeichen ist das Kennzeichen eines in der Ausbildung befindlichen Kadetten der Kadettenausbildungseinheit für Offiziere. **A3** Kriegsdienstuniform mit neuer Baskenmütze und schwarzem Plastikabzeichen. Das Luft-Wasser-Rettungsdienstabzeichen wurde erst 1943 eingeführt.

B1 Das alte, graubraune Muster der Netzausrüstung und Tropenhelm aus dem Jahre 1908. Zu beachten ist die Allgemeine Dienstmedaille. **B2** Offiziersjacke mit spitzen Manschetten, Schulterstreifen und geknöpfte Jackentaschen. Innerhalb eines Jahres wurde die runde Mütze durch die Felddienstmütze der Luftoffiziere ersetzt. **B3** Dieser Obergefreite trägt eine Wasserflasche aus dem Jahre 1925 und eine Provianttasche über ihrer Buschjacke.

C1 Dunkelblaue Hosen wurden für die Arbeitsuniform ausgegeben, die in der Regel mit gleichfarbigen, langen Baumwollmänteln, in der Kaserne getragen wurden. **C2** Winter-Rockkittel mit kastanienbrauner und hellblauer Litze, der mit dem Mantel aus dem Jahre 1936 mit farbigem Kragen und Futter, der den Status angab, getragen wurde. Zu beachten sind außerdem die medizinischen Abzeichen am Kragen. Die Sturmmütze hatte imitierte aufgeklappte Spitzen vorn und hinten. Die erste birgt das standardmäßige Offiziersmützenabzeichen. **C3** Die WAAF Offiziere basäßen nur Dienstuniformen bis zur Mitte des Krieges.

D1 Die Dienstuniform wurde zusammen mit graubrauner Archivdienstnetzausrüstung, Gasmaske und Provianttasche getragen. **D2** Dicker Baumwollköper mit bedrucktem Abzeichen. Er ist mit einem Sten Mk II Gewehr und No. 18 Funkradiogerät ausgestattet. **D3** Khakifarbene Kampfuniform der Armee wurde von vielen RAF-Abteilungen am Front benutzt. Die bestickte Version des Kombinierten Operationsabzeichens wurde von Marineeinheiten in dieser Position getragen.

E1 Overalls aus weißem Baumwollköperstoff waren in den ersten Kriegsjahren sehr beliebt. Vorderansicht einer Lebensrettungsjacke aus dem Jahre 1932, die hier gelb gestrichen wurde; getragen wird ein B Helm, Mk. IV Schutzbrille, D Maske und Stiefel aus dem Jahr 1936. **E2** Eine blaugraue Kombinationsuniform mit khakifarbenem Drillich unter dem schweren Diensthemd. Er hat eine/n E/D Helm/Maske mit Mk. VA Fliegerbrille, Gemsenlederhandschuhe und Stiefel aus dem Jahr 1941. Die Mk. I Rettungsjacke ist im alten 'flap'-Stil gehalten. **E3** Später wurde der blaue Pullover für Luftbesatzungen unter der Dienstuniform getragen, sowie die 1941 ausgegeben Schutzhandschuhe und die 1943 ausgegebenen Fluchtstiefel.

F1 Innenansicht eines GQ Fallschirmspringeranzugs. **F2** Der gesamte Fluganzug; kombinierte Muster wurden in Flugzeugen mit offenen Gewehrpositionen benutzt, und Stiefel aus dem Jahre 1930. **F3** Der Irvin Harnischanzug mit intern eingebauter Lebensrettungsschwimmblase.

G1 Dieser Bordschütze wurde mit einem 'Bag Everhot' (immerwarmer Beutel) in jedem Stiefel und mit Chemikalien geheizte Schutzhandschuhe aus dem Jahre 1940. Er verfügt zudem über einen brustartigen Fallschirm, eine Rettungsweste 'Flap Type', einen tragbaren Sauerstofftank Typ D Variante 3. **G2** Elektrische geheizte Kleidung des Typs D, die über Rayon-Unterwäsche getragen wurde; weißer Pullover der Luftbesatzung und Anzug. **G3** Ein Taylor Schwimmanzug mit elektrischer G Typ Heizung in gut erkenntlichen Farben gehalten sowie angeschlossener tragbarer Sauerstofftank MK II.

H1 Viele Flugbootbesatzungen trugen auf langen Einsätzen Kopfhörer anstelle der Helme und trugen keinen Fallschirme oder Sauerstofftanks. Die gut erkenntliche Maske ergänzte die aufblasbare Schwimmweste. **H2** Flugmontur besteht aus Shorts und Buschjacke mit Typ 4 Aertex Helm, einer G Maske und eine entspiegelte Mk. VIII Brille. Er trägt Wildleder-'Mosquito'-Stiefel und eine Machete, eine Wasserflasche und einen Revolver. **H3** Kombinierte Flug/Fluchtanzug, der für den Fernen Osten entworfen und im Frühjahr 1945 ausgegeben worden war. Der Anzug war aus Baumwolle mit einem Gürtel aus Juteleinen und Leder für Waffen. Eine spitz zulaufende Mütze mit rotem Baumwollflanellfutter und Moskitonetz waren ebenso standardmäßig.